A CONVERSATION WITH AMBASSADOR WALTER CURLEY

A CONVERSATION WITH AMBASSADOR WALTER CURLEY

Interviewed by Richard Jackson
November 30, 1998

Diplomatic Oral History Series
Association for Diplomatic Studies and Training

Walter J.P. Curley

To order additional copies of this book, contact:
Xlibris Corporation
1-888-795-4274
www.Xlibris.com
Orders@Xlibris.com

63602

CONTENTS

to my *chers collegues* with admiration and warmest wishes

FOREWORD

The ADST Diplomatic Oral History Series

For more than 230 years, extraordinary men and women have represented the United States abroad with courage and dedication. Yet their accomplishments in promoting and protecting American interests remain little known to their compatriots. The Association for Diplomatic Studies and Training (ADST) created the Diplomatic Oral History Series to help fill this void by publishing in book form selected transcripts of interviews from its Foreign Affairs Oral History Collection.

The text contained herein acquaints readers with the distinguished service of the Honorable Walter J.P. Curley as U.S. Ambassador to Ireland from 1975 to 1977 and to France from 1989 to 1993. We are proud to make his interview available through the Diplomatic Oral History Series.

ADST (www.adst.org) is an independent nonprofit organization founded in 1986 and committed to supporting training of foreign affairs personnel at the State Department's Foreign Service Institute and advancing knowledge of American diplomacy. It sponsors books on diplomacy through its Memoirs and Occasional Papers Series and, jointly with DACOR (Diplomats and Consular Officers, Retired), the Diplomats and Diplomacy Series. In addition to posting oral histories under "Frontline Diplomacy" on the website of the Library of Congress, ADST manages an instructional website at www.usdiplomacy.org.

PREFACE

The conversation that follows took place in Manhattan several years after I had returned from a four-year diplomatic posting to France. My interlocutor, Richard Jackson of *The Association for Diplomatic Studies and Training* in Washington, posed the questions which, along with my responses, were recorded on tape.

There had been no rehearsal, no pre-viewing of the questions. Mr. Jackson and I had preferred that format. It provided genuine spontaneity—at the sacrifice of time for reflection and perfect parsing.

Aside from fixing a few typos, there have been no major corrections or rephrasing of the subsequent written text. The ADST has now offered the opportunity to tidy-up the actual manuscript for publication; having been an *oral* history project, however, it seemed more appropriate to let the narration go forth naked.

I was pleased by the solid professional and personal insight that the ADST brings to its purposes. Preserving and understanding American diplomatic history is an essential obligation for us all: How can we know where we are *going*, if we do not know where we have *been*.

New York City   Walter J. P. Curley
July 4, 2009

FROM FOX CHAPEL
TO IWO JIMA AND BEYOND

Q: This is an oral history interview with Ambassador Walter Curley conducted in his office in New York City on November 30, 1998 by Richard Jackson. Mr. Ambassador, you grew up, I believe, in the Pittsburgh area. Is that correct?

CURLEY: I did. I grew up in an area called Fox Chapel, which in the days I was there as a young boy, was countryside, more or less suburbia. But I think you asked what was the genesis of my interest in foreign service. I'd have to go back a little bit there—if that's fair—to be accurate. I went to a boys' school in Pittsburgh called Shadyside Academy, which, for a western Pennsylvania institution, was relatively sophisticated. We had good French teachers; we had geography professors. Our minds were stretched. And then I was sent away, not reluctantly, but I had little say in it. I was just sent off—with very little explanation—by my parents to Philips Academy Andover. And there again, Andover had some exceedingly good windows to the world, which I was certainly entranced by.

From there I went to Yale—another step up in sophistication. I was interested in languages. I was interested in foreign area studies. I had been abroad both with my parents and with relatives and on my own with some schoolboys, so that I knew Europe and was relatively savvy as a schoolboy. This would all be prior to World War II. Just prior to the outbreak of the war, I was in Germany and Italy and saw the massing of the German force before it went into Poland. I was in Germany in 1938, so all those events stirred in me an interest in foreign affairs.

That was prior to going to Yale. I came back to Yale, majored in foreign area sociology, and then the war happened. This is a long answer to your question, Dick. I then became a Marine Corps officer. I went to boot camp in Parris Island in 1943. I was in the class of 1944 at Yale, but in the final year they sped us up, so we had our summer vacation and actually graduated in 1943.

I went directly to boot camp and from there to Quantico, where I was commissioned a second lieutenant, and from there out to California, to Camp Elliott, from Camp Elliott to Camp Pendleton. I later went to the Marine Corps base, where I joined the Fifth Marine Corps Division and went to Hawaii and eventually to Iwo Jima. We'd built up our training group and our attack force on the island of Hawaii, and then went to Iwo. I was a platoon leader on Iwo Jima, a sad but successful occasion, as you know. I lost a lot of the men in my platoon. It was a reinforced platoon. That was very, very wrenching and had an impact on my view of world affairs, of course. From a worm's-eye view, a second lieutenant's view.

I then went back to Hawaii with the Fifth Division and was tapped to be a general's aide. I became a temporary aide de camp to General Keller E. Rockey, who was at that point commander in chief of the Third Amphibious Corps. He had been commanding general of the Fifth Division on Iwo. Our mission was to go to Okinawa after having been in Guam for several weeks beforehand. Okinawa was another horrendous battle. I was not a platoon leader there, so did not have quite the deadly exposure, but I got enough front-line experience there too.

At the end of Okinawa, we went back to Guam. The bomb was dropped, and our mission, which was to attack mainland Japan, was changed to the occupation of North China: The Third Amphibious Corps moved to North China. I had taken Japanese language at Yale, and then had been sent to a Japanese language school at Camp Pendleton. So I had been assigned, as a Japanese language officer and platoon leader during the Iwo Jima battle, to getting Japanese out of caves. That was one of the jobs. So as a platoon leader and kind of a language officer, I had this experience of dealing directly, on an unfriendly basis, with enemy troops on Iwo and Okinawa.

I was also able to use my Japanese in China with General Rockey. I was transferred over as aide to General W. Arthur Worton, who was chief of staff of the Third Amphibious Corps. Worton spoke Chinese fluently; I spoke Japanese between fairly and badly. Rockey chose Worton and two other men—one was a Nisei and one an intelligence colonel—and myself to fly into occupied North China. A big part of our job was to arrange for the arrival of our troops in China two months later. So there were four of us plus two enlisted men. We flew to Shanghai from Guam, were met by the Chinese Nationalist group, and then were flown up to North China, where we were received coldly by the Japanese. Then started the long process of repatriating the Japanese occupation troops and eventually accepting their official surrender. We were also, very importantly, occupying North China as a buffer against Mao's troops in Manchuria until Chiang Kai-Shek could get his act together in the South.

All of these events—there's a litany of events here—reinforced my stirrings of interest in international affairs. North China was an amalgam, a potpourri of many, many kinds of interests, many different ethnic groups, and certainly political groups. There were White Russians, there were Red Russians, there were Chinese obviously, there were Japanese, there were Manchus, there were Tibetans. There was everything you could think of. And also the Portuguese community.

There were some French, there were some British, and some Belgians, Germans, Italians, Swiss—not lots of them, but some. It was a truly cosmopolitan arena in which all kinds of interests were at stake. Of paramount interest, of course, was our own, the U.S. interest. But working with General Worton and with General Rockey and all the problems we faced there, I'd say, reinforced my keenness to somehow after the war get into that business. The Marine Corps provided a cauldron of experience for me.

Q: How had you happened to decide on Japanese studies at Yale? That was an unusual choice.

CURLEY: That's a good question. It was before the war, so the Japanese threat was there, but it was sort of muted. We didn't talk much about it. There was a most interesting Japanese professor there who was half French and half Japanese. His name was René Yamamoto, but he was called René Meyer. His mother was a French Jew. He was a most seductive, in the intellectual sense, chap. And so he said, "Don't you people know that the great languages in post graduation period for you will be the Oriental languages?" And he said, "If you had one to choose, I would recommend Japanese." He had a silver tongue and a very charming manner, so I signed up. It was an interesting choice.

THE BUSINESS WORLD, PROTOCOL, AND MONARCHS IN WAITING

Q: So then you came back from the war years, and went to the Harvard Business School.

CURLEY: I came back directly from China. I took an aircraft carrier from Tsingtao to San Diego, and that was the repatriation of First Lieutenant Walter Curley. Somewhere after, just before I got out, I became a captain, so it was Captain Curley by then. I told my father of an interest I had in taking the Foreign Service exam, and my father, who was an interesting and sympathetic supporter and friend and just a very good guy, said, "I want you to do what you want to do." And I said, "Well, I want to take the Foreign Service exam." He said, "Go ahead and do that." I took the preliminary exam in Boston and passed. But he said, "I'll tell you what you do. Just do me one favor." He said, "Do you know how to read a balance sheet?" And I said, "Well, not really." I was, as I mentioned, a major in sociology and English and all those things that were far from a balance sheet. Well, he said, "I don't care whether you become a Foreign Service officer, a businessman, a tap dancer, a nuclear scientist, or a beach bum, but whatever you do, before you do it, at least learn to read a balance sheet, and it might serve you in good stead, somehow, somewhere." I said, "Okay," and he said, "Go to the Harvard Business School." So I did.

I had had no leave time at all. I just got out of the Marines and I found myself working my tail off up at the Harvard Business School. At the end of one year, I was fed up. I said to my old man and to my mother, "I believe I need to go find myself." That expression, which may play today, didn't play too well then. My father said, "Look, if you want to find yourself, go find yourself in some other academic or work-oriented atmosphere. I don't want you out there contemplating your navel." I said, "Well, what if I went to the University of Oslo?" I'd read about some program in Oslo. Dad said, "That sounds fine to me." And I said, "Don't worry about it. The GI Bill of Rights will pay." I was motivated by a little romance, too: I had a friend at Barnard College, and I persuaded her to come along. She took a leave of absence from Barnard, I took a leave of absence from the Harvard Business School, and we went, by boat, to the University of Oslo in Norway.

By the end of that time I guess I had found myself or something. I was recharged and had had a good time up there in Norway. I majored in foreign trade—majored, I mean, the semester I was there. It was all done in English and the foreign trade aspect was interesting. I took a little Norwegian language, liked the people enormously, got more interested in international trade, felt refreshed, came back, went back to the Harvard Business School and finished quite fascinated by business.

So I got sidetracked, sort of. I said to the old man, "I still want to be in the foreign area, but maybe not the Foreign Service. I'd like to be in the foreign trade area somehow, something with a foreign orientation." And he said, "What about the international oil business," which he had been very interested in. So I joined the California Texas Oil Company, Caltex, and my wife and I—she'd gone to Vassar—the Barnard girl had fallen behind—and my wife and I, whom I'd known and admired for many years—we'd grown up in Pittsburgh together, her maiden name was Mary Taylor Walton—geared up and went to India for four years with Caltex. At the end of that period I was shifted to Italy, where Caltex was in partnership with Fiat. And at the end of that additional four years in Italy—incidentally, we learned Italian, a lovely language, and we had by then three children, all of whom spoke Italian—we came back to New York, where Caltex's headquarters were, and we were gearing up to go to London where Caltex had a joint venture with an English company called the Regent Oil Company.

That was a most interesting prospect, but I ran into an old friend that I think you may have known of—I know he was a friend of your father's—called Charlie Brown. He was ex-CIA. Charlie was a partner of John Hay Whitney, who had founded the first venture capital firm, called J. H. Whitney and Co., where your father was one of the original partners. Charlie Brown introduced me to Jock Whitney and to Benno Schmidt, who explained the attractive qualities and attributes of the venture capital world, and my eyes danced in my head. So I left a lot of good friends at Caltex and got into the world of venture capital with J. H. Whitney and Co., thanks to your father's friend Charlie Brown and Jock and Benno Schmidt, whose son, Benno, Jr., was one of our recent—in the last 10 years—presidents of Yale. I joined J. H. Whitney and Co. in 1959, and stayed there for 15 years. However, I never lost my interest in the Foreign Service. I was a governor of the Foreign Policy Association, and I loved to keep up my Italian. I spoke French lamely, and I tried to improve that a bit; I always had the latent interest. But I was very much engaged in the venture capital world at that point.

Q: Your CV shows you wrote two books. I don't know whether they were in that period.

CURLEY: I did. Yes. Incidentally, while I was a partner at J. H. Whitney and Co., the then mayor of New York, John V. Lindsay, came to me. He was an old friend of mine. We were classmates at Yale and very close. He was the mayor at a very interesting time in New York's history. He had a lot of commissioners who ran various jobs, and one was the Commissioner of Public Events and Chief of Protocol. It was a job with two hats; it had a staff of about 30 people who did all kinds of things—interesting things. Lindsay asked me if I could take a leave of absence and become Commissioner of Public Events and Chief of Protocol for his administration. Well, I asked Jock Whitney, and Jock said, "How much do you get paid? You have a job here." I was a partner by then. J. H. Whitney and Co. was a partnership; there were only seven partners. "What would you be doing with John?" He liked John. And I told him that my pay was a dollar a year plus a big black limousine. And Jock laughed and said, "Well, go ahead and do it, but be sure you come back in no longer than a year an a half." Lindsay had asked me if I would stay until he left, which was about that stretch. So I said to John, "When you go, I go." I took a leave of absence from Whitney.

This is a long answer to your question about the books. During that period, I had assembled the letters I had written my family. My mother had died in 1958 of cancer. She was only 57. It was a dreadful loss to us. She was a marvelous person. I assembled the letters and edited them to a certain extent and gave them to my father; they were published by a Marine Corps association, and the book was called *Letters from the Pacific*. That was one book. Also, I had been fascinated during my exposure to Europe by the monarchical system of government, and always had in the back of my mind writing a book about the royal claimants and pretenders to the empty thrones of Europe.

In that period, the same period when I was Commissioner of Public Events, I had this running project of interviewing all the out-of-work kings. I did it on my own time, by letter at first, then in person. And it took some doing, because I had to be introduced and then try to seem credible to these claimants. There were 11 of them. I interviewed them all, and I wrote a book called *Monarchs-in-Waiting*. And it was published by Dodd, Mead here in the United States—and successfully, I'm happy to say. Then I was approached, or my agent was approached, by Hutchinson, which is probably the biggest publisher in the UK; so it was published there, much to my delight. It was supposed to be a pretty good read, not just a recitation of who are they (it was that as well), but also where are they and what are their chances. I started out writing with a tongue in my cheek; I thought I would be interviewing geezers or fuddy-duddies or fantasy freaks. I came to chide and left admiring. I met no fools. They were all people of real substance, of intelligence, of interest, and of ethical standards. Those royals, their families, and their claims were also relevant to history and even to today's political scene in some areas. I was fascinated by the result of inquiry. And that again fostered my interest in foreign affairs.

EMBASSY DUBLIN

Q: So the Lindsay period ended. You went back to J. H. Whitney, and then on from there to Dublin in 1975.

CURLEY: Well, here again, I don't know how much detail you want.

Q: As much as you want.

CURLEY: Well, let me comment on my appointment as ambassador, how it happened. To me at least, this is an important point: among a lot of people—and probably including yourself because you couldn't help it, as a Foreign Service officer—there has always been sort of a feeling among you career people about interlopers, political appointees or so-called non-professional ambassadors. I take some exception to that view. I know your point, and I understand and sympathize, but I take exception with the use of the word or phrase *non-professional* because a lot of the political appointees are certainly non-career but they're not non-professional. I mean I considered myself in the business world a total professional. So we like to think that when we're tapped to do a job in the government that we don't come as non-professionals. We like to bring whatever professional qualities that we have learned. So *non-career* as a phrase is okay; *non-professional* I don't like.

At that time, I was not involved in politics in any way. The only financial contribution I ever gave was a local thing, both to Democrats and Republicans. My friend, John Lindsay, from a Republican, had become a Democrat, and I gave him a little help in his campaign, but nothing, no serious money. As far as my nomination for ambassador to Dublin, I knew my subject, the subject of Ireland, because in 1958 my father and

I had bought a house in Ireland. And, very importantly, back at Yale, my senior thesis was written on the subject of "The Influence of the Irish on American Politics," and the part two of it was "The Problems in Northern Ireland." So by the time of, say, 1974, while I was still at J. H. Whitney and Co., we had already lived in Ireland for a number of years. And my wife is an historian. She knew Anglo-Irish history. I did, too, and my interests went back to my Yale days. I did know my subject.

The incumbent ambassador, appointed by Nixon, who'd been there for six years, was Moore, John D. J. Moore. I knew him well as a friend. He was older than I was; he was an older Yale grad, and a fellow member of my Yale Senior Society. I knew him in that sense. And I knew his family. He came to me one day at J. H. Whitney. He said, "I'm going down to Washington next week to tender my resignation. I haven't told them yet." He said, "My wife has died." One of his daughters had also just died, both in Ireland. He said, "I want to ask for an immediate leave of grief followed by my resignation and retirement." But he said, "I'd like to put your hat in the ring." I said, "Well, John, that's really nice of you." He said, "I won't do it unless you're interested, because they won't like it. They won't proffer it if they don't expect a definite 'yes.'" I said, "Let me check with my wife," which I did, and she said, "Are you out of your mind? It would be wonderful!" I asked Jock, who had been ambassador to the Court of Saint James, and he said, "Don't miss the opportunity if it arises." So I said later to John, "Sure, put the hat in the ring." But I added, "I have no political strength. I am a Republican, but I've done no political work. I haven't contributed anything." Well, it was right after Watergate, so Moore said, "That's all the better."

I was approached soon after we met and was asked to come down to Washington. Henry Kissinger, whom I did not know then, interviewed me. He said, "Vhat [What] are your political contributions, Commissioner?" And I said, "Well, this may be the end of the interview, but as far as any financial contribution goes, basically none at all." And he said, "Very good, very good." In those days, just after Watergate, that was the way it should be. Kissinger said, "We want clean-as-a-hound's-tooth here." So I was a political innocent in that sense, and eventually got the job and got to Dublin. That's how that happened.

Q: That's fascinating. You probably went through some period of preparation in Washington, through a course with other ambassadors.

CURLEY: I did. It has become a more formalized and broader process now, that "Charm School," so-called, that all ambassadors go to, whether they're career or non-career, whether they've been ambassador before or not. In 1974-5-6, the same period I was in Ireland, we had that program in Washington, a very thorough one, but not quite as structured as it is now. But it was good. It was very good. I did that program prior to leaving for the Dublin post. It was definitely useful.

Q: In Dublin you find a small but very effective embassy, professionally.

CURLEY: The first question a lot of people ask is: "Oh, you were ambassador to Ireland." Big smiles spread over their faces. "So you've been on a three or four year picnic." It was intriguing for me because I knew the subject, as did my wife, Taitsie. Ireland is a very interesting place, as you know, historically, intellectually, and politically. Dublin was stimulating, made all the more so in our time because of the revolving presidency of the EC [European Community]. Ireland had the presidency the year I got there as ambassador, which turned Dublin into more of a cosmopolitan place. We had a fascinating time there—not only for that reason, but that was one of the reasons. Also, 1976 was our Bicentennial Year, and the Irish, as you well know, have a lot of transatlantic affection. So that Bicentennial Year became a big deal. Also, at work there at that time was a new phenomenon that wasn't helpful. That was the Irish turn of face.

The Irish had been turned historically towards the New World—all those immigrations, the immigrants that went from Ireland to the United States by the millions—and the United States was where the Irish looked for help and inspiration and protection and familial ties. Gradually that changed into practically an about-face, when the Irish turned to Europe and were more and more considering themselves not as an extension of the UK or America or even of themselves, but really as Europeans. They were Irish first, but they were very much recognizing and relishing the fact that they were European, not American-oriented. That was an important thing that was happening to the Irish at that time.

SOVIET PRESSURES, AFFILIATIONS, AND BAD DAYS IN THE NORTH

It was also the Cold War, and my dealings with the Soviets were tricky. The Soviets had a big, big embassy there, and the riveting question was why did they need so many in Dublin? In those days, U.S. embassy personnel in Ireland totaled about 60—only 20 of whom were American. The USSR embassy had about 100—and they were all Russians! Well, you can imagine why. They had all kinds of nefarious activities going on in that embassy. It was an espionage center and clearinghouse. I used to try, and succeeded a little bit, to kid my Soviet counterpart: why did he have such a great, big embassy there? How many Soviet tourists are there a year that come to Ireland? And what's the trade balance between Ireland and the Soviet Union compared to tourism and trade with the United States? That used to make him smile, but he didn't like it. There are 33 million Americans of Irish extraction. How many Russian-Irish are there?

It was a difficult time, during the Cold War, for our relations with the Soviet Union in Ireland. Also, the Irish would try to dance their way through the tricky competing interests of the Soviets and the United States and had a tough time doing it. That made it a complicated scene there, plus the problems of the North. Since 1969, they'd gotten worse. By the time I was there, the bad days were back, and they hit an apex of pain when my best friend, among the diplomatic community there, the British ambassador, was assassinated. His name was Christopher Ewart-Biggs. He had been DCM in Paris before that, a very able diplomat and a nice guy—a good friend of mine. He was blown up by the Provos, by the Provisional IRA, in his car with his driver, by a bomb. Sad and disgusting.

So Ireland—back again to our long answer to a good question about Dublin—did we enjoy our time there and what was it like? It was fascinating; it was difficult. I like the Irish; I like the way they think. There are many different kinds of Irish, all kinds—Irish-Irish, Anglo-Irish, Norman-Irish, Protestant Irish, Catholic Irish, all kinds. It was a most interesting assignment. Let me mention my own house there—my father and I owned it fifty-fifty. When he died in 1970, I got his half. The house, built in the early eighteenth century, is on the West Coast, in County Mayo near Westport. It's on the Atlantic. So when we had time we would try to escape the rigors of duty in Dublin and go to our house in Mayo. Garrett Fitzgerald was the foreign minister during my posting in Ireland. He eventually became prime minister. The president at the time was a man called Cearbhall O'Dalaigh, who was an academic, and the prime minister was Liam Cosgrave. They were good men—and we had good, effective years there.

Q: You had a lot of interest in Ireland from Washington. There were senators and a very important constituency for Irish-American relations. We had Senator Kennedy, theoretically under Helms.

CURLEY: There's a lot of Washington affiliation there, at least ethnic affiliation, or heritage. Senator Kennedy came. I wouldn't say often, but he was there. I would see him. And his sisters came often. Jean Kennedy Smith, who eventually became ambassador to Ireland, was there. And Pat Lawford, whom I knew years before—I knew Jean before, too. They would come. Speaker Tip O'Neill, who was the epitome of an American-Irish official, never, never came. But one time I heard he was heading to Poland with a Congressional delegation, and I sent word back: "It seems to me that you ought to drift by." So he came and brought his delegation, had his daughter with him and his wife and others. They came to Dublin, and I was really glad to see him. He said, "I'm embarrassed to say I've never been to Ireland. I give a lot of speeches, and I play the role of an Irishman in Boston, and they all eat it up. But now I can go home with my head up because I've been actually here." So we had the joy of that, plus a round of golf together at Portmarnock.

We also had the lack of joy in dealing with what was perceived to be a lot of money being received by the IRA from Irish-American sources. The U.S. monies that were coming in were buying arms. And the arms were being bought from Libya; they were being bought also from Czechoslovakia and Yugoslavia; wherever they could find them, they were buying. So, surreptitiously the British Secret Service, the FBI, the CIA, the Irish intelligence service, the Irish military—and, of course, myself—all colluded to find out exactly how much money was coming in. There were ways to do that, not all successful. But we tried to apply some effective restrictions, and I think it worked pretty well. We did it for about two years, and at the end of the two years—there were ways of measuring these things, but it was not a fine science—I figured that the flow of money to the IRA was reduced down to a million dollars a year, and then it dwindled more after that. So I think we got it down to less than a million.

Q: There've been periods of tension between the embassies in London and in Dublin at different times. In your time, how was that relationship? Were there slightly different interests, or were you on the same sheet of music?

CURLEY: Very happily, serendipitously. There were three American ambassadors in London while I was in Dublin. There were Elliot Richardson and Anne Armstrong, who were good friends of mine, and there was Kingman Brewster, who was a close friend. So I had their ear at all times, and they certainly had mine. If we had any kind of problems, I'd be on the phone. It was very helpful to have that connection. The strains between the Irish government and the UK, I'd say, were just chronic, but not extraordinarily so. The assassination of the ambassador, of course, was an anomaly in some ways. Right after I left, as you know, the Queen's kinsman, Lord Mountbatten, was assassinated, so these violent flares were symptomatic of the problem, but I wouldn't say that they escalated onward after that; they were sort of spikes of violence, and then it went back to just the plain, old-fashioned level of violence. I don't mean to sound cynical or calloused.

Q: Did you have a decent staff? You had a DCM that worked well with you?

CURLEY: I had a DCM whose name was Jack Rendall, and Jack Rendall, a career Foreign Service officer, was first class, *first* class. And happily, not only professionally did we get along, but personally. We were a good team. He had a very good sense of humor, he had an analytical mind. He was a varsity smoker. He made Humphrey Bogart look like a non-smoker. And he was a total gentleman, too; always very well dressed, very well spoken, very articulate. He could drink more vodka martinis than you could possibly imagine and never turn a hair. His eyes were never bleary. His speech was never slurred, nor was his mind ever slurred. He kept that vodka well under control. But his capacity for smoke and martinis was a mere footnote. He did a fine job.

BUSH FOR PRESIDENT

Q: Mr. Ambassador, all good things come to an end, and you then left Dublin after three years. Is that right?

CURLEY: I did. After President Carter was elected, we could hear the *swoosh* of departing ambassadors of any Republican tinge. Anne Armstrong left immediately. They all left. I was waiting for the other shoe to drop, and it didn't. I waited and waited, and I made a few surreptitious calls to Washington: "No, no, no, hang on there, you never know, you never know," said my informants. And so I said to my wife, "What if we were asked to stay on?" And she said, "Well, that would be fine, but I don't think it'll happen." I said, "Well, I don't either." It went on for about five months, and then I thought, "God! I've slipped under the wire here; they haven't noticed!" We were almost euphoric in our anticipation, and then, *clunk*, the other shoe, but all very nicely. It was done with a scalpel, not a sledgehammer. It's the way it goes.

So I came back to the venture capital world. Sadly, my partner and founder of the firm, Jock Whitney, had died while I was in Dublin. The Whitney partners were all very good friends of mine. Benno Schmidt, who was the managing partner, was and is one of my dearest friends. But it's difficult to go back to a partnership. When you withdraw—as you know, you must sever everything when you go in the Foreign Service—when I withdrew as a partner, I had to take my goods and leave. To get back and crank up that partnership is difficult. So I decided I'd do a solo. I'd set up my own venture capital thing and call it whimsically, "W. J. P. Curley," which I did. But I remained in close contact with the J. H. Whitney and Co. people, and I still do. If an investment opportunity comes by which is a little bit big for my bite, which would be a lot of the time, and I need a bigger bite to go onto it, then I will call them. Or sometimes if it's too small for them, they'll call me. So we still have a nice contact.

But anyway, I left Dublin, set up my own organization, which is what I'm doing right now. However, in 1978, I got a telephone call from George Bush, who had been known by a lot of people as George Herbert Walker Bush, to a lot of others as "Poppy" Bush. He had straightened out most of us years before that: "I don't like 'Poppy'; it's too cute and preppy." And he said, "George Herbert Walker Bush is fine, but it's a little long: I'm George Bush." He called me—he was an old friend—and said, "I'd like you to help me with a quest." I said, "I'd be happy to help you with it. What is the quest?" And he said, "The White House." I said, "Some quest!" So we talked, and he said, "I really would like to take a crack at it, but I'll need all the help I can get." I like him a lot, very much indeed. He had all the qualities that I admired—I had seen him over the years—and that I thought would be good in a president. So I said, "You tell me what I can do." And he said, "Well, I'd like you to run the New York State campaign." We need to get some money, among other things, and gather the thing together." So I said, "When do you have to know this? I'd like to discuss it with Taitsie." George Bush said, "Well, could you let me know in a day or so?" I talked it over with Taitsie, and she very wisely said, "This is the kind of thing you don't do in a half-baked fashion. You say 'yes,' then be prepared to go full-bore, or don't do it at all." I agreed and called George back: "You're on. Let's go."

Well, we started, and as all campaigns go, we started slowly. We tried to build up the momentum and get our team together, and so it took me a while. I had a great co-chairman named Bruce Gelb, and we put a team together, slowly, slowly, slowly, and worked on it. And then the closer we got to the nomination and the election, the harder it got, the more time. I found myself finally at the end where it was not 20 percent of my time but had escalated up to 100 percent. When he didn't get the nomination—the team was all geared up and ready—we thought, "Oh, boy, there it goes. Gone!" But then Reagan tapped him to be his running mate, so I instantly became a vice-chairman. The Reagan team took over, and all my people took subordinate positions. The Reagan group came in, and we worked with them. George invited all the Bush state leaders like me—I was also co-chairman of the national effort for Bush—down to Washington for dinner one night, and he said, "I know we fought against the Reaganites for a long time. But that's over now." The Reagan varsity team was there, too. And he said, "So everybody reach across the table and shake hands, and let's try to win this thing." Reagan was not there, but Reagan's team was there, and this was Bush's initiative to pull the team together. And we did, and of course Reagan won.

For eight years, we did that as a Reagan-Bush organization until we geared up again for George's quest. I got out my chairman hat again for the Bush campaign. Then when Bush won, he came to me with an offer. All those people like that, all those fellows who get to positions like that—as you know, Dick—all need a coterie of loyalists around them, people with no other agenda, people they can trust implicitly. They all do. Now whether it ends up being a "kitchen cabinet" or whether it ends up being the official cabinet, whatever it is, they need the trusted ones around. So Bush called me and said, "I'd like you in the administration." And he mentioned a job in Washington that was pretty fancy, and most interesting. But Taitsie and I, or Mary and I (that's her real name), didn't relish going to Washington. We like Washington—I know you live there—and I love to go there, I have a lot of friends there, but we just didn't want to move to Washington. And then Bush said, "I really want you in the administration. I need your help—you and other guys like you that I can trust." He said, "Would you come back in as an ambassador someplace?" And I said, "Well, yes, sir (by then, it was 'sir'), but only if you'll send us someplace where we can do a goddam job. We don't want to go to someplace and have just some kind of a sinecure. We're both healthy. We're both at a good age. Send us someplace where we can work our tails off. Taitsie's just as healthy as I am and just as smart, and smarter." Well, he said, "Okay, you can go wherever you like. Call your shot." And I said, "No, sir, I want to go where I'm needed." So he said, "Well, Jim Baker will call you in a couple of days." And I thought, "Yeah, sure. I won't hold my breath." And we went away on vacation. I had not worked for Bush all those years in order to get a good job. I *had* a good job. I did not seek or need a job in the Bush administration. I was happy to go full-time back to trying to make two plus two equal five in the venture capital game.

TAPPED FOR PARIS

We were down in Nassau, at the Lyford Cay Club, being really frivolous, and the telephone rang. It was Jim Baker on the phone. He chided me, saying, "We're up here working." Made me feel terrible, but he said, "The President and I would love to have you get back in the diplomatic service here, and the President says you can go anyplace you like." Boy, that was pretty nice. I said, "Jim, that is so nice, but honest to God, anyplace . . . ." He said, "Say something, otherwise it's going to be . . . ." And I said, "Well, we both speak Italian, like those Italians, and know their character. We'd love that." But I said, "That's not necessary." I said also, "We know India. We don't speak it—I have a little Tamil, but not much. Well, we'd go to India and we'd love that." Baker said, "Okay, I'll call you back in two days." And in two days, the President called me back—while we were still down there; I felt doubly embarrassed. And the President said, "How good is your Italian?" And I said, "My Italian's pretty good." And he said, "Is it as good as your French, because that's where you're going? You're going to France. How good is your French?" He and I had the same French teacher at Andover. I said, "Well, it's about as good as yours, if you had that French teacher." And he said, "Oh, no, it has to be better than that." (Well, it was. I took it at Yale and I had used it. Funnily enough, I'd used my French a lot in China. There was a French community there. So my French wasn't bad.) Well, he said, "That's where you're going." When I told Mary, or Taitsie, she was thrilled and excited and surprised.

I'm jumping a bit to the language part of it. I really worked on it before I left here. I worked with a man. I didn't write anything; we just spoke. So I got my French up to a pretty good level. It wasn't bad, but I got it up to a better level. And then when I got over there I insisted at dinner parties that we preferred to speak French at the endless formal dinner parties.

They'd always start out saying, "Shall we speak French or English?" Or they'd always start out in English. And I was dying to speak English, but I said to them, "No," and Taitsie did, too, "No, we prefer to speak French." It was agonizing at first, particularly for Taitsie, but it was very good for us both. That way I became totally at ease with that part of it as we started our four years in France. We were there '89, '90, '91, '92, and I came home in mid-'93.

Q: You followed Joe Rodgers, then.

CURLEY: I followed Joe Rodgers, right. Let me tell you a rather interesting incident. George Bush did an extraordinarily thoughtful and useful and nice thing. I had been approved by the Senate, and I had no problems there at the Senate Foreign Relations Committee hearing except with Senator Joe Biden. Joe Biden was asking me if I spoke French, and then I spoke French to him at the hearing, and asked him if he spoke French. I said it nicely. Senator Claiborne Pell was there and does speak excellent French. So Claiborne Pell asked him the same thing, and Biden was put off. I think he just wanted to bait me a bit because I was a Republican nominee. Anyway, I cleared it through with no problem. Now we were preparing to go, and Bush called me up on the phone. We were here in New York, and I had just finished that ambassadorial charm school with a lot of other ambassadors. It was very worthwhile, incidentally. "What are you doing next weekend," George Bush asked. When the President calls, where does the big gorilla sit? Anyplace he wants. I said, "What do you have in mind, Mr. President?" And he said, "Why don't you and Taitsie come up for the weekend to Kennebunkport?" He said, "I think it would be very useful because I have President Mitterrand and Madame Mitterrand coming over with a bunch of his senior people." I think it might be useful if you met Mitterrand before you got to France." I said, "If the protocol is okay, not having presented my credentials. If you think the niceties of that wouldn't be uneasy-making for the French, I can't think of anything I'd rather do." So he said, "Well, don't worry about the protocol. I'll handle that part. Why don't you come up a day early?" George Bush loves to play golf, and so do I. All the Bushes are very competitive. Bush said, "Come up a day early and we'll play a little golf with Baker and Brent Scowcroft."

So, we went up a day early and had a bit of that, and then arrived Mitterrand, Madame Mitterrand, and Admiral Langlade—remember him?—and of course, Foreign Minister Roland Dumas, Ambassador de Margerie, and a whole phalanx of French government types. And it was a time of very serious discussion but also some fun. I could never have perceived Mitterrand without a tie, or without a coat, for that matter. Well, in the Bush way of life, particularly at Kennebunkport, it is militantly casual. Sweaters were kind of foisted on and ties were snatched off President Mitterrand, and we had a hell of a good time. We had a most interesting time there that weekend, and I can tell you, if you ever want to hit the ground running and have a leg up in France, be introduced to the President of France by the President of the United States in his house with his arm around you. It sets your social and professional scale pretty well by the time you get there. Baker was there, and Susan, his wife, and Taitsie, and one of Bush's sisters, Nancy Bush Ellis, was there, and of course, Brent Scowcroft.

It was a very, very cozy time at Kennebunkport. There was a payoff, because Mitterrand knew from that and from other subsequent things that I had real access to the Oval Office and to Jim Baker. That was most helpful. Well, Mitterrand *plus* his senior people. Dumas saw the relationship between George Bush and me. So that was very helpful. Also, Bush and Mitterrand were genuinely good friends. Now that was an odd couple—I mean, it really was a funny couple, so different, but they were seriously firm friends; they genuinely liked, admired, and respected each other. That had built up during the time that Bush was Vice President. He and Mitterrand had solidified this friendship. And the reason, probably the main reason, that Bush chose me, outside of the fact that he wanted a loyalist around, was that he wanted a friendly gesture to indicate to Mitterrand that he was sending one of his close friends who'd been ambassador before and for whom he had great personal rapport. He wanted Mitterrand to know that. Mitterrand would be flattered. It works that way. So that was the basic reason I was sent to France. I was very grateful to Bush for arranging it that way.

Q: What a great start!

CURLEY: It was a good start. Yes, indeed.

Q: So you arrived, then, at that big embassy, 50 government agencies, or whatever you had there.

CURLEY: Yes. 1200 employees, a change from Ireland, at least in size or scope.

Q: You kept your DCM, Mark Lissfelt, who had stayed on.

CURLEY: As I mentioned to you before we started, I thought I'd save a little money for the State Department regarding travel expenses for interviewing prospective DCMs, so I said, "Let's start with the incumbent." So Mark Lissfelt came to New York for me to interview. I thought he was a really good person. We got on. The chemistry was just great, and I liked everything about him from the start, and as time went on, I liked him more and more. That holds true today. Both he and his wife, Cindy, are extraordinarily able, capable, nice, funny, interesting, curious, and attractive people. I enjoy them. We made a good team. And I hasten to add that when he finally had to leave, after renewing his assignment to the point of near irregularity, I was again deluged by people who wanted to replace Mark.

I got a call from Larry Eagleburger, who said, "I'd like you to take very seriously Avis Bohlen as a candidate. Think of her very seriously." And I said, "Well, Larry, I know Avis. I like her very much. But," I said, "we are already gender-imbalanced here at the moment. The head of our commercial section is a woman. All of our senior consular people—consuls general and consuls—are all women." I said, "If we have another here, it's, I think, a little *de trop [French: overboard]*. Nothing to do with ability or anything." And Eagleburger said, "Well, no, I just repeat this: take it seriously." I thought very seriously, and said, "Well, that's not a big problem, gender imbalance. I mean, think of the years we went along when there were just too many men around. It wasn't so bad. So it's not going to be so bad if we have too many women." Well, Avis came, and Avis and I became really good friends. She is without peer, peerless; she did a wonderful job, and we again were a very good team. I liked Avis and admired her enormously. And that holds true today. So I was lucky three times: with Jack Rendall, Mark Lissfelt, and Avis Bohlen. I couldn't have been luckier.

ENGAGING THE FRENCH

Q: You had some security worries in that big embassy. Did somebody sneak in at one point?

CURLEY: Starting in '89—as I said, we got there in May or June '89, just in time for the embassy Fourth of July party, an instant way to make 5,000 new friends—it was really a remarkable period in history, the events in that '90 to '92 period: the reunification of Germany, the implosion of communism in Eastern Europe, the disappearance of the Soviet Union, the Gulf War, Maastricht. We had all these things just go bang-bang-bang, one right after another. I mean it was just incredible, let alone the Tiananmen Square massacre and all that, but just in Europe itself and especially in France—not London as much. London's certainly very important; it always has been, always will be. But a lot of that activity—a lot of the repercussions and reactions and responses and intrigue, if you will—was happening in Paris. So it was a cascade of events and occurrences. Of course, the Gulf War was the epitome of that whole thing.

And that was a difficult period with the French. That was not easy. The French took to that coalition effort—putting together the coalition—very reluctantly, very. They saw themselves in that posture they always have of being outside the military structure of NATO, and there was no way they were going to get into the coalition other than as an observer. I had a lot of instructions from the Secretary of State and from the President himself: get in there and do a little shin kicking, they said. I tried, but the French were wearing shin guards. But when I was given a little "ammunition" by Secretary Baker, I went in and had a chat with Foreign Minister Roland Dumas. He and Jim Baker did not have the best of chemistry. They were both very effective people, but chemically they had a hard time. I went in to see Dumas about getting France to agree to the refueling of some of our big aircraft—bombers—that were leaving the UK en route to the Gulf. We wanted to have them refueled in southern France and then onward. That was finally agreed to, and then, kicking and screaming, the French were finally brought into the coalition. And then, as always, they did a hell of a good job. The French were on that left flank in Desert Storm; they worked with our Marine Corps, so I was particularly interested as a former Marine Corps officer. They worked well with the Marines. The French did a good job.

Q: Did the defense minister resign at that point?

CURLEY: Chevènement.

Q: Chevènement, yes.

CURLEY: He did.

Q: So it was a moment of high feelings?

CURLEY: A lot, a lot. Well, I suppose this is supposed to be all candid, and no public secrets here, but I was pleased when Chevènement resigned. He was virulently anti-American, and he was very communist. That sounds like an epithet, but I don't mean it to be. He was very much that way, very left socialist in his political orientation, and with that came this very undisguised anti-Americanism. I found that very hard to deal with, because he became kind of petulant and, I thought, a little arrogant—never so much to me, but I could see it in the reactions. I was pleased when he moved on. The French, as always, have a little problem with our way of getting at the problem, but once aboard, as historically they've done before, they've always been good partners, militarily and . . . .

Q: Your job was somehow explaining that to Washington, which didn't always see it that way.

CURLEY: Well, on that subject, if I can divert a bit here, there was a period of high sensitivity about them. Right after the victory in the Desert Storm Operation, I got a call from the White House, from President Bush himself, and he said, "I want to talk to you about the French reaction right after this Gulf War thing, because there are some things we'd like to do with the French and I'd like to talk to you about them. Could you please come back to Washington?" And I said, "Wonderful, I'd love to." I hadn't been to the U.S. all during the Gulf War. So I said, "Sure, I will do that, Sir." So Taitsie and I went back. She hadn't been back to see the kids or anything. We went right to Washington and had dinner with the president and Barbara Bush at a dinner party in the White House, not for us but including us. There were a lot of heavy hitters there: the Bakers, the Cheneys, the Websters, the Colin Powells, and about six others.

The next morning, I met alone with the president in the Oval Office. It was expected to be a half an hour, which is a long time with the president. It ended up being over an hour. And what he wanted to ask me was, what was the French national mood and the governmental mood—the man on the street mood—post-Desert Storm? I said, "Damn near euphoric." And it was true. People were stopping me on the street and saying, "*Monsieur l'Ambassadeur Amèricain [French: Mr. American Ambassador]*," and giving me a kiss, men and women, on both cheeks. I told that to Bush. And actually, it happened to me on the street and in a restaurant. I said, "The mood is euphoric. Even in the Travelers' Club, that men's club, that bastion of propriety, I got kissed by a man." The President said, "I hope it wasn't in the men's room." But it was like that. It was euphoric.

He said the reason for his keen interest in the French mood was that they wanted to get the French into the muddle about the Arabs and the Israelis. Baker was very keen, as you know, about getting on with the Middle East peace process. And he first wanted to make the French a major partner in that. They'd been out there for so many years. They were very sophisticated on the subject. But recently—or in our recent history—they'd been kind of left out of the discussion or invited only as observers. So Bush wanted to make that change, bring in the French as major colleagues. Was the time right? That's what he wanted to talk to me about. Was the time right for that? And I said, "It will never be better." Well, that ball took a lot of different bounces before landing.

But back to the French-U.S. friction. Right after that euphoria, not unnaturally, I guess, a period of irritation started, a subliminal erosion of good will. It was almost palpable, and it was not pleasant at all. There was friction and abrasion between the U.S. and French interlocutors. It was there. And in Foggy Bottom, in the State Department, there was again, to use that word, palpable anti-French feeling. I didn't go native there in France, but I could feel in Washington this feeling that the French were anti-American, and there was a knee-jerk reaction against the French in some very important quarters in Washington, in the State Department. And I could see this manifested in the negotiations that were happening, or trying to happen, in France between American teams and their French counterparts. It was really pretty bad. I could see that the American style, the instant familiarity, the back-slapping, the cold-water candor, the rush to the finish, the do-it-now approach, came eyeball to eyeball with the French *il faut réfléchir* [French: one must think about it] attitude, the Cartesian logic, the let's-take-a-little-relaxation-over-this-thing. It was a clash—nothing too fundamental, I figured—but it was a triumph of style over substance. I could see these guys—you know them all, Dick, because they were all prominent State people—some of them have left, but some of them are still there—prominent experts, State Department personages—who had this thing, not to be outdone by the French, who had the same kind of stylistic problem.

The French ambassador in Washington was a man called Jacques Andreani. And Jacques Andreani had a few stylistic problems of his own. To many, he seemed arrogant, abrasive. But I said this to him, I said, "Look, Jacques, we've got a style problem here between our top negotiating teams, our policy people. If we can get over that, we can smooth this road and get talking decently." He said, "You talk to your people." I said, "Okay," and went to the President and to Baker. Baker first. This was in Washington. I went to Washington for this purpose. I said, "I perceive problems with certain State Department people," and I named them, "at a certain level. These people are able and good and they're looking out for our best interests, but it's very abrasive, and I think we ought to try to change their style or much of our joint efforts in harmonizing policy will go down the drain." And I said, "You've got to get them to change it." Secretary Baker said, "No, you tell them to change, but you tell them I said so." I said, "Okay, and I'd like to mention this problem to the President, if you don't mind." And I did. I mentioned the guys' names and everything, but in a way that—I hope—didn't impugn their careers or anything, or their intelligence. The President said, "You tell those clowns, and if they have a question they can tell me or Baker."

So I have this instruction—I'll put it like that—and I went to three or four of them and spelled out the problem and just said, "Look, let's change the act a little bit." Well, I put myself in this and said, "Let's change our act and our style a little bit to get over this problem." And they all said, "Those French bastards are hard to deal with. You know that?" And I said, "That's exactly they way they feel, too." So I went to Andreani, and he did the same. We got it changed. And it got better. There was one day when we started to talk about it in Paris with everybody present, the two sides. And, for a little example, the French would say, "Sometimes we don't like the way you arrive in Paris on your plane from Washington and at seven o'clock in the morning we all sit down to a business breakfast. We don't like to meet until 10. We hate the U.S. 'working breakfasts.' You want to meet at 7:00." There were a lot of little things, but we got the stylistic things out of the way so we could deal properly with the bigger matters. It became amiable, at least, again for a while. I basically like the French, a lot.

DEALING WITH THE SPHINX

Q: Did you think somehow that France was in a delayed transition in those years and that all of the shocks you mentioned of the world changing around them, and particularly German reunification, had changed their role, and they were beginning to worry about millions of North Africans and how they were fitting into the society?

CURLEY: Absolutely. No question about it.

Q: Lots of their industry, particularly in the computer area, was way behind ours, and they felt threatened.

CURLEY: They did, but in the industrial part first they caught up fast, particularly on the high-tech side. They caught up very fast on the nuclear energy side. They certainly did, and surpassed us in some ways. Their main nervousness was the German problem. The immigration problem with North Africa and all of that racial, if you will, problem was very important and very nervous-making to them, but of priority importance was this fear of the German problem. I'd say I had three serious discussions on Germany with Mitterrand, and Mitterrand told me one time at breakfast, just the two of us at the Elysée, that he was very afraid of the Germans. He said, "I admire the Germans. I really admire them, but I fear them." He said—I'll never forget this, and he was very interesting on the subject, very knowledgeable, very intellectual, and learned—that he always considered the Germans as a *volk [German: people]*, not a nation but a *volk*. He said they have a feeling of their own destiny, that their destiny lies to the east, and there's always *lebensraum [German: room for expansion]*; there's always that. Our American efforts at the time had a lot of emphasis on Gorbachev, if you recall, and on Kohl and Bush; the three of them were always talking.

They were the ones in a huddle. And that made Mitterrand nervous. It made the British very nervous, too. Margaret Thatcher was a little nervous. But you're dead right. France was in a transition then, in many ways.

Q: You got off to such a wonderful start with Mitterrand from the intro, and he's often called, I think, "the Sphinx." You got to know him quite well in those years. Perhaps towards the end, he also knew that he was sick.

CURLEY: Yes, we did become friends. Mitterrand was never the type that relished the backslapping, let-me-tell-you-the-latest-joke type relationship. He had a very wry sense of humor, kind of an ironic view of life, and he could tweak you. He liked to do that in an enigmatic, intellectual way. I liked his sense of irony. He was highly intelligent, so whatever you were going to do, you had better be prepared to tap dance pretty fast, because he knew what he was talking about. He was always most gracious to my wife and to me and always interesting to listen to. And happily for my relationship, from my standpoint, if I needed to see him, I could call up and be received. I would try to keep that to a minimum, which is why, I guess, I was received—because I didn't hound him. We got along well, and I enjoyed it.

You asked me another question here. I'm trying to remember what it was.

Q: We talked about his health.

CURLEY: Big point. I was asked a number of times by Washington if I could find out what was really wrong with Mitterrand, because you'd see him sometimes and he'd look terrible, absolutely terrible—I mean, kind of yellow, parchment skin, frighteningly bad-looking, unhealthy looking—and then other times he'd be ruddy and vibrant. His demeanor was always the same. His actions and his intellectual qualities were always there, but the physical look would vary wildly. So I was asked by Washington what did I think. And of course, they had everybody on the case; they had the CIA. I was told that they figured it was kidney failure. I said, "Well, let me see what I can find out through all kinds of sneaky sources, French sources, and then you can see what you can find out." It was more than curiosity. I had a certain compassion about it. I wasn't just gleefully trying to find out what was wrong with the Sphinx. And it was an important bit of knowledge strategically for us Americans.

I made no headway. I tried everything and heard all the different things. And do you recall when there was a meeting of Bush and Mitterrand in Saint Martin, down in the Caribbean? Baker called me. I was flying over from Paris to Washington and then getting on Air Force One to fly down to Saint Martin with Baker and Bush, which I did. But before I left Paris, Baker called and asked me, "Can you find out about Mitterrand's health? President Bush is definitely going to ask me, what *is* wrong with Mitterrand and how will he be or how is he when he gets to Saint Martin?" And I said, "Okay. I will make a point of seeing him before I leave Paris, which is tomorrow." I didn't have to make a point because there was a reception at the Elysée that evening. So I went to it and there was Mitterrand big as life. I had a minute with him and talked, and he said he was looking forward to seeing me in Saint Martin. He looked perfectly wonderful. He looked terrific. So I cabled that back to Baker, and then later I spoke with him on Air Force One going down to the Caribbean. I said, "He looked just terrific, and all that worry about his health you can put aside."

Bush then goes over to a rendezvous area to wait for Mitterrand. Baker and I went out to the Saint Martin airfield to greet the Concorde that came in with Mitterrand. Baker and I are standing there at the foot of the ramp. The door opens and Mitterrand stands at the top of the stairs looking like hell, like *hell*. And Baker, out of the side of his mouth, as we're walking up the stairs and Mitterrand's walking down the stairs, says, "Ambassador, you're information is [expletive]. That man coming down the stairs isn't sick; he's dead!" And by God, he looked it. He really looked bad. We never learned what it was. Of course, it ended up being prostate cancer, but I still think (the doctors in France were never forthcoming) he also did have a serious kidney condition. I think he had dialysis, on somewhat of a regular basis, which took him from deathly pale to ruddy, and fooled us all.

Q: He came in as a real socialist, I guess, with communists in his government, and then evolved to a liberal or a very moderate position. You watched much of that process. Was that expediency or change in his outlook?

CURLEY: Expediency. Oh, yes, he was a most expedient fellow. Well, I suppose the change in outlook became expedience. Mitterrand—before I got there, but I certainly watched it before I got there—single-handedly defused and eliminated, for all intents and purposes, the Communist Party, on his own. That wasn't due to any pressure from the conservatives. No, he did that with some very adroit plays with the socialists.

On the subject of Mitterrand, as long as this is a historical document to a certain extent, or to the fullest extent, Mitterrand's personal life was something that was always an enigma to Americans, not so much to the French. But Madame Mitterrand never featured much in his official life. That doesn't mean that she was a shrinking violet. She was anything but that. She had her own agenda. She had her own passions, and I mean both physical and philosophical, and she was an interesting person, but certainly not, as far as I was concerned, a fetching person. She had minimal charm. I'm told that in previous years, way back, she'd been very good-looking. There were some vestiges of that. They also said that she'd been charming. As far as I was concerned there were no apparent vestiges of that. They also said she was very intelligent, and I would say that was in fuller bloom.

But François Mitterrand had a private life. He was a romantic figure in many ways, to put it mildly. He had many snuggles—I don't think promiscuously, not all at once—but he had a litany of liaisons with various ladies, none of whom, as far as I could discover, thought badly of him afterwards, which is about as neat a trick as you can pull—to have a former romance speaking well of you. But I think he succeeded. So that says something for him. While I was there, France elected its first woman prime minister, Edith Cresson. Edith Cresson had style—not much class, but a lot of style. She was smart and she knew where she was going, and it was rumored—France is always big on this—that she had been one of former President Mitterrand's "friends"—as *Time Magazine* used to call it, "a great and good friend." I rather liked Edith Cresson. But she was very naughty. They were great and good friends.

Well, old François was a most interesting character. That friendship with Bush that I alluded to was everywhere—in the dark days and in the bright days. That was always there. I give Bush—and Baker, of course—full credit for getting France into the coalition in the Desert Storm operation. Absolutely. I don't think enough time has been spent by historians or analysts or reporters on the matter of Bush's personal diplomacy. It's been alluded to, but I don't think it was ever properly understood, or at least the breadth of it or the depth of it understood. It was a most important ingredient in Bush's foreign policy operations and a most serious ingredient in the man himself. His effective relationship with Mitterrand is a prime example.

THE COST-CUTTING CZAR, GISCARD D'ESTAING, AND FOREIGN AFFAIRS AGENCIES

Q: Were they putting pressure on you to slim down the size of that big embassy in those years, the budget cuts? That came somewhat later, I guess.

CURLEY: Well, yes, it did. It started in my time with the cutting down of consuls, of consular staffs. I got instructions, orders, if you will. Do you remember Ivan Selin, the State Department cost-cutting czar? Bizarre—I liked Ivan, but boy, he had some very spartan, draconian ideas. Instructions came—you don't *instruct* an ambassador if you're at that level, but I got *strong recommendations*, to be followed by instructions if needed, from Ivan Selin to get rid of three consulates: Bordeaux, Lyons, and perhaps Strasbourg. I knew I couldn't fight all three battles at once, so I chose Lyons, a very important center, as you know. It is sort of the equivalent of Chicago or Pittsburgh. So I said, "No." And that raised a little hell. Selin responded, "What do you mean, 'No'?" I said, "I mean just that. You give me your rationale. Start out with numbers, because if we're talking numbers, let's play a numbers game; I'll give you some and we'll see who wins." And I went to Washington and fought with Ivan. He's a good competitor. He likes that. He relishes the battle. I won that battle, at least while I remained in Paris. I think that after I left, the closures happened quickly.

Dick, maybe an interesting—at least to me—parenthetical comment here might relate to my friendship with Giscard d'Estaing, the former president of France and, as you know, an arch-adversary of Mitterrand, a totally different type. He was from the conservative right and a very interesting man, seen by many to be Mr. Arrogance, Mr. Elegance, Mr. Supreme personified, but a most engaging man. During my time there he approached me initially and asked if he, as representative of an important French party, could be briefed. And I said, "Yes, of course." At times when I felt I was too busy or didn't want to do it, for some reason, I always did it anyway. I'd go over to his office. He would offer to come to my office, but I never accepted; he was the former president, and so I always went to his office. We became friends and, particularly during the Gulf War, he was always interested in some of the rationale that was being employed. I was as forthcoming with him as I possibly could be without revealing anything compromising. He really appreciated that, and in turn—many times rather than just hearing one party line or if I had some dilemmas in my own mind about how certain things might work—I would go to see Giscard d'Estaing about French and European matters. And we became great friends, and are to this day. Well, that was just a little postscript to my time there, but it added to my repertoire, so to speak. I never talked about it much—I didn't hide it—but I appreciated that friendship.

Q: Thinking of you sitting atop that big embassy and all those streams of information coming in to you every day, the French papers, the international press, the embassy reports, the CIA reports . . .

CURLEY: All the above and more.

Q: . . . all the above and a lot more, were there any you particularly valued? Did you develop a confidence in what the Agency, for example, was reporting? You found it useful?

CURLEY: I'm going to say something that history may think you rehearsed me for, and I can assure historians that you did not, nor did anybody. One of my abiding impressions of my years in working in that foreign service area was the quality of the intelligence of the men and women I worked with in the Foreign Service. I'm not saying that gratuitously. I experienced it; I utilized it; I exploited it. It was extraordinarily wonderful. There were exceptions always, but the average of excellence and the quality of work that I got from almost all sources was of a very high level and an enduringly high level. I was impressed by most of the agencies very much. I had no complaints. I had some irritation, some complaints, about a few internecine conflicts, like between the defense attaché and the political officer and this and that. There were a lot of those.

They had nothing to do with the intelligence level of these men, or women, but rather with whatever bad chemistry or just bad viewpoints or conflicting viewpoints existed between the parties, and I would have to wade in every now and then and do some scolding that an ambassador is supposed to do from time to time. Overall, however, the reporting was wonderful, whether it was the CIA, whether it was the DEA. I mention those two off the start because a lot of people don't know about the DEA, for example. They know about, or think they know about, the CIA—excellent. I found the little things about the CIA better than some of the big ones. I was always sort of abashed by the fact that they misread the Soviet Union's strength so badly. So I think on macro work they may need a little checking up. On some of the less macro and more micro work they were first class.

The budget cutting you asked about was going on. We always had to pay attention to that, and it got no better as time went on. That budget really shrank, and for understandable reasons, I guess. But it got worse in subsequent times. I know Ambassador Harriman faced it and now Rohatyn faces it. The State Department was and is lousy, inept, at courting and lobbying Congress for the money it needs. Lousy.

Q: Then finally came the election, and the administration changed yet again, and that would have put an end probably to that term of yours in Paris.

CURLEY: I stayed through March. New York was always our home base. We never gave up our apartment; we just, sort of, left the apartment. And my wife said that, after four and a half years away, the culture shock of coming back from Paris—*bang*—to Park Avenue and 74th Street was a little much, so she suggested that it would be a very good idea for the ambassador and his wife to take a little "decompressing" detour to Morocco, where we had never been—to your old stamping ground, Dick. So we spent 10 days there and decompressed. We traveled all over, *partout [French: everywhere]*, thanks in great measure to the loan of the ambassadorial van by Freck Vreeland, who was chief of mission there a very short period of time; he gave me his personal Land Rover. And then we got a driver who knew what was going on, a driver who had driven for Ambassador Joseph Reed and was on his own by then. So we moved about in some style and had a wonderful time.

My time in France and in Ireland—and I say this absolutely subjectively, not objectively in any way—were very lucky posts for me. They were both interesting; they were both areas that I remain fascinated with.

UNFINISHED BUSINESS AND JACQUES CHIRAC

Q: Even in France, were there any things that you regretted not getting to or accomplishing? One always leaves with a sense of unfinished business, but any particular objective that you had?

CURLEY: Yes, it remains an objective. There were some small objectives, and then there were some bigger ones. The bigger objective which still is there is this. It was there when I got there and was there when I left and will be there a long time unless something is done about it. The United States and France are ancient historical allies. The old cliché that France is America's oldest friend is historically true. We've been allies in a number of wars; we've been firm friends. But the average American on the street doesn't know beans about France or about the French. The man walking along the street in downtown Cleveland—ask him about a Frenchman or a French woman or France. What do they know? They think of a beret or they think of a song or wine or *couture* or something. They just don't understand what the hell the French are about. Strangely enough, that is relatively true—not as much, but relatively true—in France about the Americans, although we have a lot of Americans that have been over there as soldiers, and a lot of our movies and our television shows and tourism have given some knowledge of Americans over there. I'm not saying it's the right image, but some knowledge. That doesn't exist here. There are a fair amount of French tourists that come here, but not even close to the millions of Americans that go there.

Also, it was explained to me by the French—obviously, I would have cottoned on to it anyway—that there are no real French *immigrants* here. I mean, in Quebec a little or maybe a tiny bit in New Orleans, but hardly anybody has a French grandmother. Everybody has an Irish grandmother or an English grandfather or German or Jewish or whatever, but there is no French residue here. There's no "race memory," no heritage. There was no French immigration to the U.S. You see, we don't know enough about the French, and I don't think that's good. I guess there are ways. We tried. The USIS, which is an echo now, tried through cultural exchanges, and they never worked very much or very well. So that's a major project left undone: more mutual knowledge of each other in the French-American relationship. But, after all, maybe a little mystery isn't all bad. Maybe it's better that way in the long run.

Q: Right.

CURLEY: Among the short-term things that I wish I'd done and didn't do was to spend more time in *eastern* France. It's relatively unknown to the average American. There's a lot of power there, with a lot of industry, a different kind of mentality. I know a fair amount about it, but not enough. That's something I wish I'd done more of.

Q: There's been a lot of writing about what they call "bananas" these days, that the regions of Europe are assuming more powers than the states, and that there are industrial regions that stretch, say, from Barcelona up through southern France and to Milan and then in Germany.

CURLEY: Yes.

Q: Does that correspond to what you see?

CURLEY: Absolutely. That was one of the reasons that I objected most vociferously to closing the Lyons consulate, because Lyons is right in the heart of one of those big belts you're talking about. So I thought that would be just madness to close a consulate in an area like that. No, I think that's very true, and increasingly so, don't you?

Q: Very much, very much.

CURLEY: I did not mention—and should have—President Chirac. Now Chirac was mayor of Paris while I was there and had been prime minister, as you know. He and I became good friends, too. I always liked him, Chirac and his wife, Bernadette. She's charming and gracious and fun, and I liked *him* very much. He's very different from Mitterrand in the sense of *homme d'état [French: statesman]*. I'd say Mitterrand was definitely an *homme d'état*. I'm not too sure that that same expression applies to President Chirac. He's certainly literally an *homme d'état*. He's President of France! But Jacques Chirac does not have that certain imperial gravitas. He has *other* fine and crucial qualities. I mean, I can see Mitterrand's face on a coin, and I'll tell you the person who also could see his face on a coin or a stamp very readily was Mitterrand himself. Sometimes when you looked at him he'd turn his face in profile. He had a feeling, I felt, that he was the emperor, and he had that imperial kind of view of life: François le Quatre [French: François the Fourth]. I don't think Jacques Chirac thinks of himself as a head on a coin. He's a little more relaxed in that sense, but a very nice man, a first-class mayor, having his problems as president in that "cohabitation," but a thoroughly nice man, a great admirer of America, and very understanding about the frivolous things of America. He's very tolerant, unlike Minister of Culture Jack Lang or his ilk, who take great exception to the so-called American culture invading France. Chirac's much more relaxed about that; he likes Big Macs and chocolate sodas and things like that, junk food. A good man, and I think an effective politician. I wish him well. We shall see whether the "style factor" raises its ugly little head between our two governments.

Q: Well, Mr. Ambassador, I know you've got a one o'clock appointment. This has been a very interesting interview, and unless you have anything further you'd like to add, we thank you.

CURLEY: Well, you are very welcome, and I'm flattered that you took the time to come up and see me. I hope we meet again.

Q: Thanks very much.

PRESIDENT GEORGE H. W. BUSH'S PERSONAL DIPLOMACY

Private comments by Walter J. P. Curley
Excerpted from discussions at Hofstra University about
the Bush Administration
April 17-19, 1997

I have been pleased to note that recognition of George Bush's personal diplomacy has resonated throughout various commentaries on his administration made in very recent years, and I am happy to comment briefly on my own experience with that particular style of leadership which directly affected my responsibilities as chief of mission in France.

Let me say first of all that I think an awareness of the early influences on George Bush is essential for an understanding of the later president of the U.S.

I first met the Bush family in 1938 when I was a student at Andover. Over those years of friendship I had many occasions to see the family dynamics at work. Good spirits prevailed at the Bushes' house; everybody talked, but everybody also listened. It was conversationally competitive.

And it was competitive in other ways. The Bushes respected excellence in any field. They all 'strove'; they aimed to excel.

Leadership was a natural companion to the Bush sense of competition. The Bushes seemed to have no "side", no pretense. They liked earthy jokes, and always relished a good laugh. The Bushes also respected dignity; on occasion, they could be unwittingly courtly, or outrageous comedians.

The Bushes valued friendship enormously. It pervaded their entire approach to life. I didn't see George Bush during World War II, although we were both in the Pacific—respectively as Navy and Marine Corps officers—nor right after the war when we were both in the oil business, he in Texas and I in India.

Not even later on in the mid-1970s when we were both ambassadors, he in China and I in Ireland. We corresponded a bit, but seldom met.

In 1978, however, after we had both returned to private life, George Bush called to ask if I would help his effort in seeking the presidency. For the next fifteen years we worked together politically, i.e., until 1993, when we both left our posts. During those years I saw vividly the effects of those earlier influences on his life.

There was something quintessentially "American" about George Bush's up front candor and informality. This particular American quality does not travel well to all countries, but Bush's brand of it did. He made friends and he kept them.

This quality of reciprocal loyalty characterized George Bush's relationships with his colleagues in government as well as with his peers abroad. With his staff there was a collegiality, laced with a feeling of purpose and a compulsion to "get it right."

The cascading events in the early part of the Bush administration had, obviously, tremendous impact on France, and put urgent pressure on the President's personal diplomacy, at home and abroad. The warm rapport with François Mitterrand, the President of France, for example, that had begun during George Bush's time as Vice President, had grown into an important friendship.

The two presidents were an unlikely couple, but their mutual respect sustained the French-American relationship through some very rough weather. Telephone calls between the two of them were a fairly regular occurrence, and the issues ranged from prickly to white hot. There is, for instance, no doubt in my mind that President Bush's personal diplomacy made possible the eventual French participation in the Desert Storm coalition.

At first, the French came tentatively into the Gulf War as partners. The initial negotiations with the French put hard strains on our bilateral relationship. Even later there was simmering French reluctance in principle and in strategy. (As one example, I dealt with Foreign Minister Roland Dumas on the sensitive issue of permission for the landing and refueling in southern France of our big bombers en route from the UK to the Persian Gulf.) But eventually the French forces joined the coalition against Iraq, and did so effectively, thanks in great part to President Bush's—and, of course, Secretary Baker's—personal interventions.

I should mention that my own initial introduction to the French in my official status was organized by President Bush in a most thoughtful way. Two weeks before my wife and I left for our post in Paris, President and Mrs. Mitterrand came to spend the weekend with Barbara and George Bush at their house in Kennebunkport. President Bush invited us to join them. We stayed in the house with the Mitterrands, the Bushes, Jim and Susan Baker, and General Brent Scowcroft. The others in Mitterrand's entourage—Foreign Minister Dumas, Admiral Langsade, Jacques Attali, Ambassador de Margerie and the others—were billeted in the village along with Secretary Baker's principal counselors from the State Department. It was a weekend of substantive discussions plus some fun.

I must say, if you want to be set up well when you get to Paris, have the President of the United States introduce you in his own house to the President of France, with his arm around you! It was an enormous help to me professionally; it indicated, to the French President and to his senior colleagues, my access to the Oval Office and to Secretary Baker. This awareness was extremely useful throughout my term in France. On the strength of the strong private rapport between Bush and Mitterrand, the French president summoned me several times to express strong feelings which he knew I would convey, complete with nuances, directly to Secretary Baker or to the Oval Office. François Mitterrand, a fascinating and very private man, valued highly his personal karma with George Bush.

My personal friendship with President Mitterrand, catalyzed initially by the comradeship between the two heads of state, was a great bonus for me. He was always extraordinarily gracious to Mary and me. From time to time the French President invited me alone (usually for breakfast) for a strategic tour d'horizon, and also received me promptly at my rare request.

The Bush personal diplomacy was always in evidence in dealings with his ambassadors. A nasty problem of cultural contrasts between French and

Americans interlocutors developed in '91-'92. These irritating differences were causing a triumph of style over substance which made the official relationship more prickly than it should have been.

During that highly destabilized period, French-U.S. discussions took on a definite edge. There was a subliminal erosion of good will. In Washington there was undisguised anger at certain French positions; negativism in respect to the French was almost endemic at Foggy Bottom. French official attitudes were seen as intransigent and "anti-American." The French in Paris, of course, felt the same way about our side. These abrasions were most visible at the mid levels of the State Department and the Quai d'Orsay, and not so obviously at the presidential level, where civility still prevailed. After several months of clashing styles, discussions had turned into snappish exchanges, and suggestions had become threats. The American penchant for automatic familiarity, instant solutions, cold-water candor and confrontational negotiation had come eyeball-to-eyeball against French formality, Cartesian logic, and Gallic procrastination.

I conferred with the French Ambassador in Washington; we agreed that the atmosphere could be brightened by mutually recognizing our various ethnic allergies and by getting some of our principal foreign policy bureaucrats to change their acts, or at least to adjust their styles.

I identified certain senior U.S. officials whose abrasive attitudes were most apparent, and in some cases notorious (even if understandable). I explained my concern to Secretary Baker and to President Bush, who went to bat. I got the president's permission, with the secretary's cooperation, to whisper a few words of "suggestion" into the ears of these American officials. French Ambassador Andreani then made his own moves regarding the style problem at the Quai d'Orsay. It all seemed to work: the atmosphere and attitudes brightened perceptibly.

In my own experience, instances of effective personal diplomacy by George Bush occurred continuously throughout his term in the White House. The early family influences were much in evidence. As in other capitals and strategic areas of the world, the presidential friendship, support, and extremely effective personal diplomacy of George Bush were always there for me, his man in Paris.

www.ingramcontent.com/pod-product-compliance
Lightning Source LLC
Chambersburg PA
CBHW061220280526
45784CB00006B/2565